Slithering Snakes

PYTHONS

GAIL TERP

BLACK RABBIT BOOKS

Bolt is published by Black Rabbit Books
P.O. Box 3263, Mankato, Minnesota, 56002.
www.blackrabbitbooks.com

Marysa Storm, editor; Grant Gould, designer;
Omay Ayres, photo researcher

Names: Terp, Gail, 1951- author.
Title: Pythons / by Gail Terp.
Description: Mankato, Minnesota : Black Rabbit Books, [2021] | Includes bibliographical references and index. | Audience: Ages 8-12 | Audience: Grades 4-6 | Summary: "Diagrams, graphs, and fun text help readers explore the habitats, diets, and daily lives of pythons"- Provided by publisher.
Identifiers: LCCN 2019026813 (print) | LCCN 2019026814 (ebook) | ISBN 9781623102746 (hardcover) | ISBN 9781644663707 (paperback) | ISBN 9781623103682 (ebook)
Subjects: LCSH: Pythons–Juvenile literature.
Classification: LCC QL666.O67 T44 2021 (print) | LCC QL666.O67 (ebook) | DDC 597.96/78-dc23
LC record available at https://lccn.loc.gov/2019026813
LC ebook record available at https://lccn.loc.gov/2019026814

Special thanks to Jessica McCarthy for her help with this book.

Printed in the United States. 2/20

Image Credits

Alamy: Ken Griffiths, Cover; Peter Maszlen, 6; iStock: damaloney, 12; Minden Pictures: Ignacio Yufera, 15 (middle); Mary McDonald, 24–25; Michael and Patricia Fogden, 15 (top); Michael D. Kern, 22 (top); Peter Blackwell, 13; Newscom: Peter Stachiw/ZUMA Press, 21; Science Source: ANT Photo Library, 24, 32; Shutterstock: Adam Brice, 4–5; Africa Studio, 27 (mammal); Alan Tunnicliffe, 18; Aleksandr Sulga, 27 (human); alfotokunst, 9; Angel Simon, 27 (lizard); Checubus, 27 (wild dog); Chris Watson, 1; Eric Isselee, 10–11; fivespots, 3, 27 (adult python); Heiko Kiera, 15 (btm); John Mitchell, 28 (top); Kuznetsov Alexey, 11; Liz Boynton, 27 (young python); Pakhnyushchy, 27 (rodent); Runa0410, 17, 22 (silhouettes); Sanne vd Berg Fotografie, 28 (btm); Stephen Mcsweeny, 27 (hawk); viper345, 31; Yuri Schmidt, 16–17
Every effort has been made to contact copyright holders for material reproduced in this book. Any omissions will be rectified in subsequent printings if notice is given to the publisher.

CONTENTS

CHAPTER 1

Pythons in ACTION

It's night. A giant python waits by an animal trail. **Prey** should be coming by soon. The python is ready. Its heat sensors will tell the snake when warm bodies come near. Some rats run by. They're too small for the hungry snake. It waits for larger prey. Something big is coming. When it gets near, the python sees it's a big, tasty antelope.

Time to Feast

Once the antelope is close enough, the python strikes. It bites and holds the antelope with its teeth. It coils its powerful body around the prey. The snake squeezes tightly. After a few moments, the antelope's heart stops. Now it's time to eat. The python opens its jaws wide and begins to swallow the antelope whole.

Blending In

Pythons are powerful **predators**. There are about 40 kinds of pythons. They all kill prey by **constriction**.

These snakes come in many colors, patterns, and sizes. The skin of most pythons is marked by spots and bands. But some are a solid color. Each type of skin is just right for the snakes' **habitats**. The snakes blend right in.

16 to 33 feet (5 to 10 meters)
16 to 23 feet (5 to 7 m)
3 to 6 feet (1 to 2 m)
up to about 2 feet (.6 m)
5
10
15
20
25
30
35

PYTHON FEATURES

SMOOTH BODY

HEAT-SENSING PITS

EYES
FORKED TONGUE

Large meals last pythons a long time. The snakes can go weeks or even months between meals.

CHAPTER 2

HUNTING and Homes

Pythons eat prey that fits their size. Large pythons eat antelope, pigs, and other large **mammals**. Small pythons go for smaller prey, such as rodents and lizards.

Where Pythons Live

Pythons live in Africa and Asia. They also live in Australia. These snakes can be found in a wide range of habitats. Some live in forests and grasslands. Others live in rocky places or swamps. They can be found on the ground, in the water, and in trees.

ROCKY PLACES

GRASSLANDS

SWAMPS

WHERE PYTHONS LIVE

Python Range Map

Tens of thousands of Burmese pythons now live in Florida.

Invaders

Pythons aren't from the United States, but many now live in Florida. The snakes started off as pets. Some of them got too big for their owners. Their owners released them into the wild.

These huge snakes have taken over their new habitats. The pythons eat **local** animals, including pets. Some of the animals they eat are **endangered**. And there aren't any large predators to stop the snakes.

CHAPTER 3

FAMILY Life

Pythons live alone unless it's time to **mate**. Some pythons mate every year. Others mate every two to three years. Mating season depends on the type of python.

After they've mated, females lay eggs. They then coil around the eggs. While on the eggs, some mothers shiver. This movement helps the eggs stay warm.

Until their eggs hatch, mothers don't eat. The eggs hatch in about two months.

COMPARING SIZES

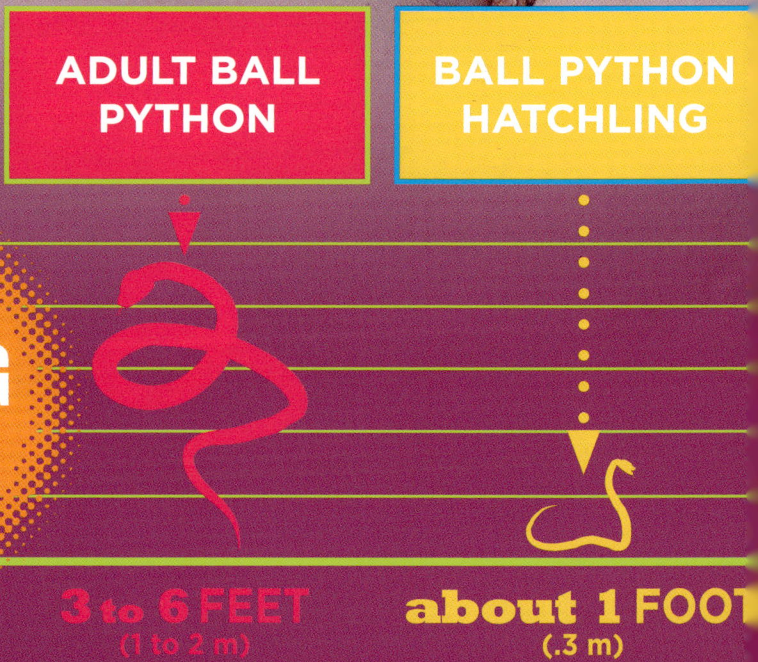

Hatchlings

Once they hatch, the babies slither off to find their first meals. They are **independent**. Their mothers don't have to care for them. They're ready to catch, constrict, and eat prey.

BY THE NUMBERS

ABOUT 100
HOW MANY TEETH A PYTHON HAS

about 30 MINUTES
HOW LONG BURMESE PYTHONS CAN HOLD THEIR BREATH UNDERWATER

up to 100
number of eggs females can have at one time

20 to 25 years

LIFE SPAN
(all kinds)

up to 200 pounds
(91 kilograms)
HOW MUCH A BURMESE PYTHON CAN WEIGH

CHAPTER 4

Part of THEIR WORLD

Most adult pythons are big. They have few predators. But their young have quite a few. These include hawks and wild dogs.

Humans are a threat to pythons of all sizes. They trap pythons to sell as pets. They kill them for food or their skin. People are also destroying python habitats. These snakes don't have as much room to live.

Python Food Chain

This food chain shows what eats pythons. It also shows what pythons eat.

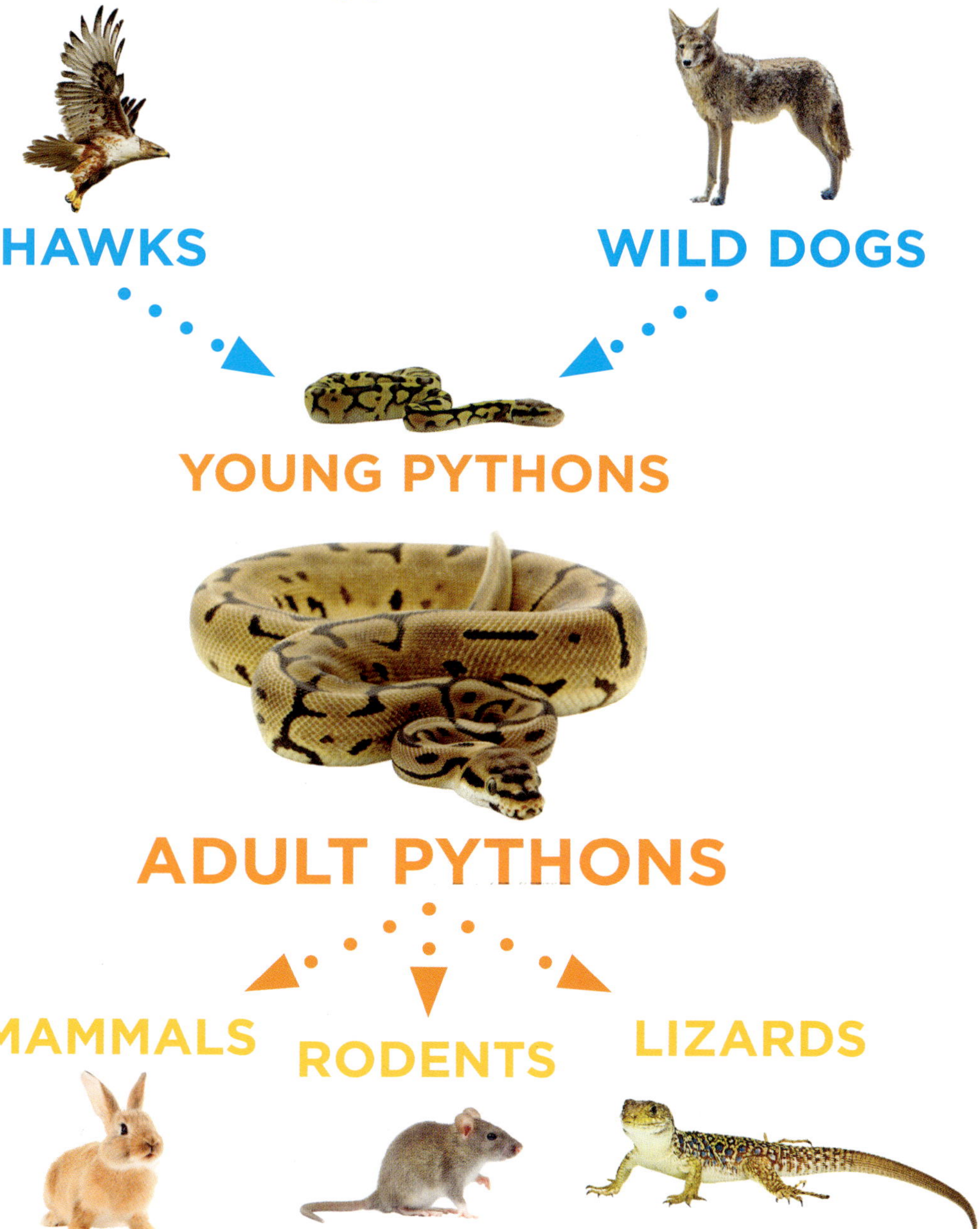

If danger is near, ball pythons curl up in balls. Curling up protects their heads from attack.

Protecting Pythons

Some kinds of pythons are in danger. Their populations are decreasing. Some countries, such as Australia, have rules and parks to protect them. Parks give pythons a safe place to live and hunt.

Pythons play a key role in their habitats. They help control rodent populations. Their young provide food for other animals too. It is important for people to protect these incredible animals.

GLOSSARY

constriction (kuhn-STRIK-shuhn)—the act of making something narrower, smaller, or tighter

endangered (in-DAYN-jurd)—close to becoming extinct

habitat (HAB-uh-tat)—the place where a plant or animal grows or lives

independent (in-di-PEN-duhnt)—not relying on anyone or anything else

local (LOH-kuhl)—a person or thing who lives in a particular area, city, or town

mammal (MAH-muhl)—a type of animal that feeds milk to its young and usually has hair or fur

mate (MAYT)—to join together to produce young

predator (PRED-uh-tuhr)—an animal that eats other animals

prey (PRAY)—an animal hunted or killed for food

LEARN MORE

BOOKS

Ciletti, Barbara. *Burmese Pythons*. Invasive Species Takeover. Mankato, MN: Black Rabbit Books, 2017.

Holmes, Parker. *Pythons on the Hunt*. Predators. Minneapolis: Lerner Publications, 2018.

Messner, Kate. *Tracking Pythons: The Quest to Catch an Invasive Predator and Save an Ecosystem.* Minneapolis: Millbrook Press, 2020.

WEBSITES

Burmese Python
kids.nationalgeographic.com/animals/burmese-python/#burmese-python-tree.jpg

Python
kids.sandiegozoo.org/animals/python

Python Snakes
www.dkfindout.com/us/animals-and-nature/reptiles/pythons/

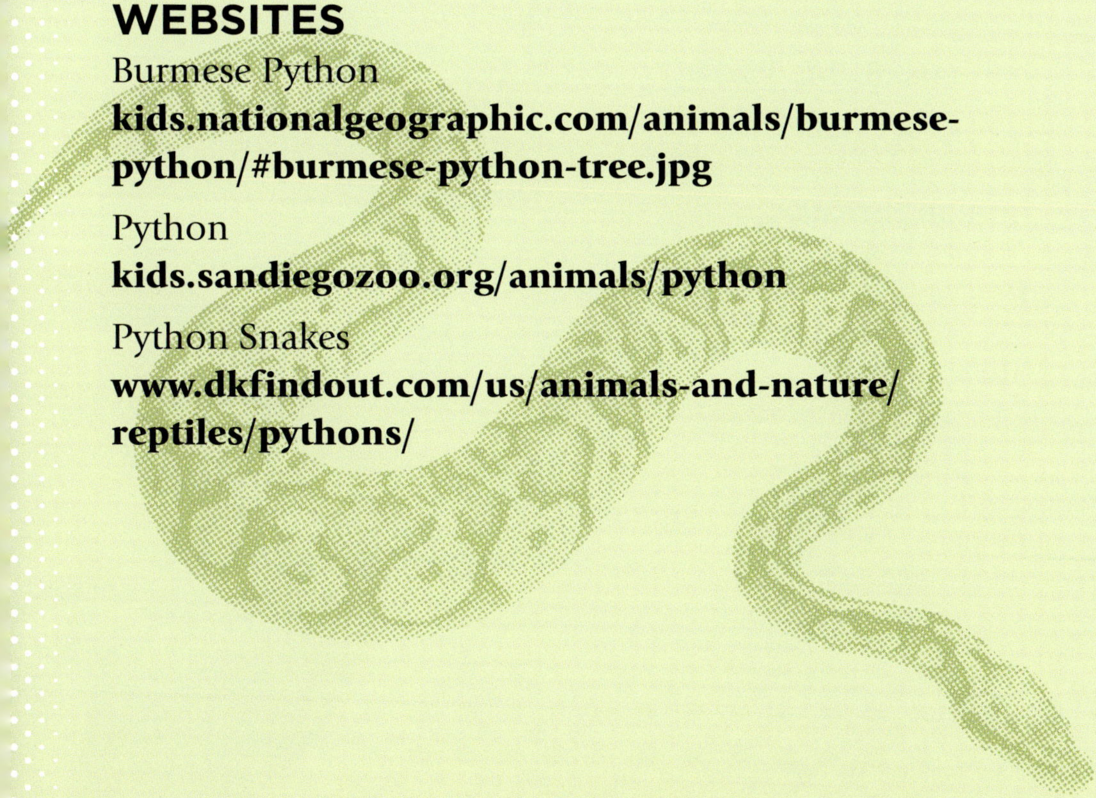

INDEX